6B

1/16

D1104915

Severe-Storm Scientists

Chasing Tornadoes and Hurricanes

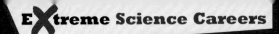

Extreme Science Careers

Severe-Storm Scientists
Chasing Tornadoes and Hurricanes

Jennifer Way and Timothy R. Gaffney

Enslow Publishing
101 W. 23rd Street
Suite 240
New York, NY 10011
USA
enslow.com

Published in 2016 by Enslow Publishing, LLC
101 W. 23rd Street, Suite 240, New York, NY 10011

Library of Congress Cataloging-in-Publication Data
Way, Jennifer, author.
Severe-storm scientists : chasing tornadoes and hurricanes / Jennifer Way and Timothy R. Gaffney.
    pages cm. — (Extreme science careers)
Summary: "Discusses careers in storm science, including education, training, specialties, and salaries"—
Provided by publisher.
    Audience: Ages 12+
    Audience: Grades 7 to 8.
    Includes bibliographical references and index.
    ISBN 978-0-7660-6968-8
1. Severe storms—Juvenile literature. 2. Storm chasers—Juvenile literature. 3. Meteorology—Juvenile literature.
I. Gaffney, Timothy R., author. II. Title.
QC941.3.W39 2016
551.55—dc23
                        2015011327

Printed in the United States of America

To Our Readers: We have done our best to make sure all Web site addresses in this book were active and appropriate when we went to press. However, the author and the publisher have no control over and assume no liability for the material available on those Web sites or on any Web sites they may link to. Any comments or suggestions can be sent by e-mail to customerservice@enslow.com.

Portions of this book originally appeared in the book *Storm Scientist: Careers Chasing Severe Weather.*

Photo Credits: © All Canada Photos/Alamy, p. 59; © AP Images, pp. 12, 33, 52, 94; Carsten Peter/National Geographic/Getty Images, p. 14; © Chris Alan Selby/Alamy, p. 37; © City Image/Alamy, p. 43; Courtesy, D. Gary Hufford, p. 46; Daniel J. Cox/Oxford Scientific/Getty Images, p. 101; Danita Delimont/Gallo Images/Getty Images, p. 107; David Boyer/National Geographic/Getty Images, p. 41; David Greitzer/Shutterstock.com, p. 55; © Dennis Hallinan/Alamy, p. 70; Dorling Kindersley/Getty Images, p. 97; Education Images/UIG via Getty Images, p. 21; George Jansen, Colorado State University, pp. 34, 38; Greg Wood/AFP/Getty Images, p 64; Herb Stein, Center for Severe Weather Research, p. 25; © iStockphoto.com/Ole-Sarge, p. 18; Jerry Kobalenko/All Canada/ Getty Images, p. 110; Jim Edds/Science Source/Getty Images, p. 73; Jim Reed/Science Source, p. 3; Jim Reed/ Science Source/Getty Images, p. 20; Joe Readle/Getty Images News/Getty Images, p. 10; JOHNSON LIU/AFO/ Getty Images, p. 75; Justin Sullivan/Getty Images News/Getty Images, pp. 9, 11; Kenji Arimura/Moment Select/ Getty Images, p. 85; Ladislav Nemec/isifa/Getty Images, p. 80; Lowell Georgia/National Geographic/Getty Images, p.92; Michael D. Lemonick/The LIFE Images Collection/Getty Images, p. 39; Michael S. Quinton/National Geographic/Getty Images, p. 49; Photo by Luc Rainville (APL/UW), pp. 98, 100, 103; Photo Courtesy of Brian Russel, pp. 83, 84, 88; Photo Researchers/Science Source/Getty Images, p. 29; © RGB Ventures/SuperStock/Alamy, p. 78; © Rob Crandall/Alamy, p. 56; Roger Hill/Barcroft USA/Getty Images, p. 90; Ryan Etter/Ikon Images/ Getty Images, p. 6; Ryan McGinnis/age fotostock/Getty Images, p. 22; Samuel D. Barricklow/Stone/Getty Images, p. 23; solarseven/Shutterstock.com, (chapter heads throughout book); Sylvre SELBONNE/AFP/Getty Images, p. 68; Timothy A. Clary/AFP/Getty Images, p. 87; Tinker Air Force Base History Office/NOAA Photo Library, p. 16; © University Corporation for Atmospheric Research, p. 62; © US Navy Photo/Alamy, p. 105; Wolfgang Kaehler/LightRocket via Getty Images, p. 48.

Cover Credits: Jim Reed/Science Source (launching weather balloon).

Contents

Chasing storms is an exciting and, at times, dangerous job. The men and women who follow severe storms put in a great deal of work and preparation to ensure their safety.

Chapter 1

Chasing Knowledge

O n May 29, 2004, an intense storm swept across western Oklahoma. Wind kicked up the dust, while rain beat it back down. Although no human eye could see it yet, a tornado was forming. Dr. Joshua Wurman had an electronic eye trained on the storm, using a special radar unit that was mounted on the back of a truck.

Joshua Wurman is a scientist who hunts tornadoes. His mobile radar unit is a special tool he made to help him hunt them. The radar unit emits radio signals and measures the echoes that bounce back. It can measure wind speeds and directions inside a storm, including the mysterious, whirling funnel of a twister. It even lets him study what is happening inside a tornado, the way a doctor might use x-rays to peer inside a patient's body.

This storm was a brute. "It was a storm [that] was very windy and kicking up a lot of dust," Wurman recalls. "We couldn't see. We had several vehicles in our fleet, and we told everybody to stay away, and we went into the storm . . . with the radar."[1]

By 2004 Wurman had seen and studied tornadoes and violent storms more closely than most scientists. But violent storms could still spring surprises. This one was about to.

"We parked [the truck] in front of the tornado, about two to three miles [3-5 km] away, and started scanning it [with the radar unit]. That's the usual thing we do. We'd get in front of it and let it come towards us, and at a certain time when it got too close, we would run away. . . . The tornado got less than a mile from us, so we said, 'All right, time to move.'"

Wurman was sealed inside a tiny cabin between the radar and the driver's cab. He was concentrating on the radar data that flowed across a computer screen. But he could tell something was wrong outside.

"We're driving south, and it's clear we're not moving on the highway. I'm yelling at my driver in front, saying, 'We can't stop here. We've got to keep moving. There's a tornado coming at us.' And he's yelling back at me, telling me he had the [gas pedal] floored, and we weren't going anywhere."

The tornado came right at them. Thanks to the radar, Wurman could see it: a tight funnel of wind whirling at 130 miles (209 km) an hour. But the radar

A homeowner sifts through the remains of his property in El Reno, Oklahoma. A series of tornadoes devastated the area on June 1, 2013.

was detecting an additional threat that only later study would make clear: the truck couldn't move because the storm surrounding the tornado was packing winds of up to 180 miles (290 km) an hour!

"The door got ripped off our truck. Stuff got ripped off the roof. It was getting bad quickly, and we couldn't figure it out, and we couldn't get out of it because we couldn't move the truck."

Scientists who study weather have many high-tech tools and gadgets at their disposal. Space satellites observe weather from above the atmosphere. Instruments at remote stations around the world tirelessly

Torandoes near Oklahoma City were responsible for overturning cars and causing damage to homes and businesses.

The 2013 tornadoes of El Reno, Oklahoma, slammed this plane into a building. Eight people died as a result of the tornadoes, including several storm chasers.

report weather conditions. Supercomputers crunch massive amounts of data that can help predict the weather and track changes in Earth's climate.

Sometimes the only way to understand weather is to get right into the middle of it—and that is precisely what some scientists do. These brave scientists leave behind the laboratory and put themselves in a truck chasing tornadoes, in an airplane flying through hurricanes, or in a primitive hut on the remote Arctic ice.

Pursuing the knowledge these scientists seek can be a thrilling adventure. It can also be hard, dangerous work that is anything but glamorous. In the chapters that follow, the stories you will read are not just entertaining

A weather balloon is released in Steamboat Springs, Colorado. It will provide meteorologists with useful information about clouds at different altitudes.

tales. The dangers these scientists face are real. A flight through a hurricane is more frightening than fun, after all. And a charging bear is a serious threat.

The scientists' desire to learn, though, pushes them past their comfort zones and helps us all. The more they learn about weather, the better meteorologists can predict dangerous weather and warn us about it. The more they learn about Earth's changing climate, the better we can understand how climate change will affect us—and how we are affecting it.

Dr. Joshua Wurman is a meteorologist who tracks storms like this tornado. He sees tornadoes and hurricanes as exciting opportunities for exploration.

Chapter 2

Nature's Fury

What motivates someone to become a storm scientist? Are they looking for excitement, or for a unique way to help others? Dr. Joshua Wurman thinks it is a little bit of both. "We want to understand the unknown. It's that drive to explore [that] humans just have. . . . The drive to explore and learn things. [And] we want to do good, basically. It sounds corny, but we're trying to study things that will have some value. We study storms so we can forecast them better and warn people better."[1]

Tornado forecasting is not a new field. The National Weather Service credits the first tornado forecast to predictions made by two Air Force weather officers on March 25, 1948. Five days after a tornado ravaged Tinker Air Force Base in Oklahoma, Captain Robert C.

Miller and Major Ernest J. Fawbush correctly predicted that weather conditions were ripe for more twisters. As storms developed and swept toward the base, they issued a tornado forecast. Their forecast gave people time to make sure that loose equipment was secured, air traffic was warned away, and people took shelter. Sure enough, a tornado roared across the base, causing $6 million in damage, but no loss of life.[2]

Small, Rare, and Short-Lived

Scientists have been trying to improve tornado forecasting ever since that famous first forecast. But even after more than half a century of research with

Tinker Air Force Base in Oklahoma was hit by a tornado in 1948. Thanks to accurate forecasting, no one was killed.

ever-better technology, scientists still have much to learn about twisters.

A big reason is that tornadoes are elusive. "They're small, they're rare, [and] they're very short-lived. If you see a tornado and decide you're going to drive towards it, often by the time you get there, it's over," Wurman says. Even if you get close to one, it is hard to tell what is going on inside it. "You can't go there. You can't see it."

Wurman has experienced firsthand the need for better tornado forecasting. On May 3, 1999, he found himself chasing tornadoes that threatened Norman, Oklahoma, where he lived—and where his wife and baby were at home. His team was racing south through Oklahoma City toward Norman, following the storm. Recalling the scene as if it were happening, he says, "Pieces of wood and insulation and stuff are falling on the road, so we know it's chewing up homes. It's a very bad tornado. . . . It was heading towards Norman, and I was trying to call my wife and say, 'Get out of there.'"

The tornado missed Norman, but Wurman recalls the path of destruction it left in Oklahoma City. "We were driving through neighborhoods that had been destroyed. It was pretty shocking. My memory of it is [that] everything was brown, because all this mud and dirt had been thrown around. Nobody was out there. Power poles were down. People had been killed. We had no idea what the scope of it was. We just kept driving. We were still going after the tornado. That was our job."

The funnel of the tornado is the thin tunnel that reaches from the cloud to the ground. The tornado's strong winds extend much wider than the funnel itself.

What Causes a Tornado?

A tornado is a violent, rotating column of air that reaches from a thunderstorm down to the ground. As a thunderstorm develops, a change in wind direction and speed can cause the air in the lower atmosphere to spin sideways, like a rolling log. Then the rising air within the thunderstorm tilts up the rotating air. A rotating column of air two to six miles (three to ten kilometers) wide now extends through much of the storm. Most strong and violent tornadoes form within this area.

Tornadoes can occur in many parts of the world, but they turn up most frequently in the United States, east of the Rocky Mountains, during the spring and summer months.[3]

The Central Plains are prime hunting ground for tornadoes. A part of this region sees so many twisters that it is known as "Tornado Alley." Tornado Alley includes parts of Texas, Oklahoma, Kansas, Nebraska, and other states. The land is basically flat, so cold, dry air from the north can meet warm, moist air from the Gulf of Mexico. Wurman says a third factor is air that flows off the Rocky Mountains and forms a cap that bottles up the energy in the air below it. When the cap can no longer contain that air, "there's so much energy it's almost explosive," he says. This is when storms are most likely to form tornadoes. These conditions are most common in the springtime.[4]

A research meteorologist tracks storm activity on his computer.

"There are other areas of the world that have tornadoes, but they tend to be less violent and much less frequent," Wurman says.

On the Hunt for Tornadoes

Weather forecasters can predict when tornadoes are likely, but they still cannot say precisely when and where a twister will appear. When Wurman heads out for a day of tornado hunting, he knows he is likely to return empty-handed.

Just as Batman has the Batmobile, Wurman has the DOW. That is short for Doppler on Wheels. The DOW

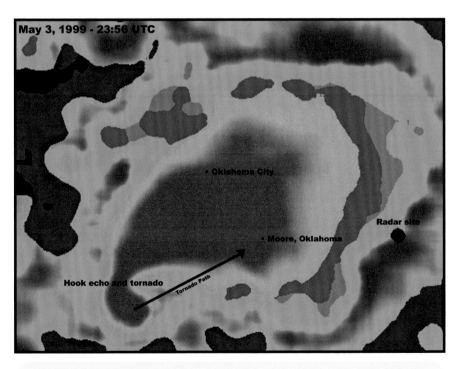

Meteorologists use Doppler radar to determine where the strongest storm activity is located.

is a truck equipped with a special kind of radar unit called a Doppler radar. By bouncing radio signals off raindrops, bugs, or dust suspended in wind, a Doppler radar unit can measure the wind's speed both toward and away from the radar.[5]

A tornado-hunting expedition may last several days, with meals eaten on the road and nights spent in motels. Wurman travels with a small support team in the DOW as well as an SUV. Wurman calls the SUV "a geekmobile" because it is equipped with radio antennas and other weather instruments. Wurman's team uses it as their

A mobile Doppler radar truck scans a storm to measure its wind speed.

A supercell thunderstorm barrels through Tornado Alley in Kansas. Supercells are known for producing tornadoes as well as hail the size of golf balls.

scout car. It can run ahead to check road conditions and find parking spaces for the truck, or it can dash close to a tornado, check air temperature and pressure near it, then speed away—something the truck, heavy with radar gear, can't do as well.

Some people have made a business of chasing storms. They lead tours across the plains, their customers hoping to glimpse a twister. Sometimes groups follow Wurman's hard-to-miss DOW. However, Wurman downplays the adventurous side of his work. "I can't say it's exciting because we're so busy doing what we're doing. There's a lot of stress associated with picking the right part of the state, picking the right county, picking the right storm, getting on it at the right time, making the right road choices. Amateur chasers are probably having a lot more fun than I am when I'm leading the fleet out there."

Sometimes Wurman gets excitement he could do without. Being pinned down in the 2004 thunderstorm was one of those times. He did not know it then, but the winds blowing around the tornado were fiercer than the funnel itself.

"We just turned the truck into the wind," he recalls. That made it the smallest possible target for flying debris—and the approaching twister. "The tornado got within half a mile of us and then turned in another direction. But we couldn't have done anything."

An Explorer Inside the Storm

Joshua Wurman is a scientist, but he is also an explorer. "A hundred years ago, I'm sure I'd be on a boat, looking for new islands, or continents, or something," he says. "Sometimes I think it's a loss, but that sort of discovery is all done. There are no more continents, or islands, or rivers left to discover. There are still places to discover, going down into deep-sea trenches and places like that. . . . Inside tornadoes, inside hurricanes, places like that are among the last places to explore."

Wurman uses his Doppler on Wheels (DOW), a truck with a special radar unit, to study tornadoes.

A Deadly Chase

Getting a closer look at storms is exciting, but dangerous work. Unfortunately, chasing storms can prove deadly. On May 31, 2013, Wurman and his team were following a tornado in El Reno, Oklahoma. This massive twister was about 2.6 miles (4.2 km) wide, the widest ever measured on Earth. Wurman's team was clocking wind speeds of around 250 miles (402 km) per hour using the Doppler on Wheels.

The El Reno tornado killed eighteen people, including three professional storm chasers. Although the chasers had many years of experience and strived to observe storms as safely as possible, storms take unpredictable paths. Wurman's team may have survived because their radar picked up the movement of a rare anticyclonic tornado (a tornado moving in reverse) within the larger storm. "I'm very happy my team had a radar out there. We only knew about [the anticyclonic tornado] because of the radar; otherwise we may have driven into it." Storm chasers like Wurman realize that while their knowledge helps them detect danger, there is always an element of luck in evading it safely.[6]

Wurman received a bachelor of science degree in physics and interdisciplinary science from the Massachusetts Institute of Technology (MIT) in 1982, but his interest soon turned to weather science. "Meteorology has some very big, interesting problems [that] you can see every day. What makes a tornado?

What makes lightning? What causes climate change? All those things are very in-your-face kinds of problems. My feeling was they can be tackled by mere mortals." He continued his studies at MIT to earn a master's degree in meteorology in 1982 and then a doctor of science degree in meteorology in 1991.

His first research job was with the National Center for Atmospheric Research (NCAR) in Boulder, Colorado. NCAR is a research center managed by the University Corporation for Atmospheric Research. This is a group of more than one hundred universities that pool their research dollars to tackle projects that are too big for any one of them to pursue alone. NCAR also gets some research money from the federal government. In return, NCAR research helps the government learn better ways to predict dangerous weather.

It was at NCAR in 1994 that Wurman got the idea of putting a Doppler radar on a truck to chase down tornadoes. He started raising money and gathering hardware. He continued to work on it when he took a job as a professor at the University of Oklahoma in October 1994. He built a lot of it himself, with help from graduate students and his wife. He started using it the next spring.

Wurman still remembers the first time he aimed the DOW's radar antenna at a tornado. Suddenly, he could see the twister in "thousands of times" more detail than he had seen before. "I just remember looking at my [radar] screen, and I was just shocked. It was amazing."

Mobile Weather Radar Units

Mobile weather radars were a novelty when Josh Wurman built his first storm-chasing Doppler on Wheels in the mid-1990s. Since then, the number and types of mobile weather radar units have multiplied. Government agencies and universities around the country have mounted different kinds of radar units on trucks to study weather. Each one is a little different from the others, but they have the same basic parts: a flatbed truck; a radar antenna mounted on a turret, which allows an operator to turn or tilt the radar while the truck is moving or parked; and a box-shaped control cab that houses the radar's electronics, computers, and other gear.[7]

Wurman says using the DOW is "like having a microscope. You look at pond water [with a microscope] and you see all the things in pond water. . . . Every place we look with these mobile radars, we see new things, some of which we expected, some of which we don't understand."

Careers in Weather Science

A weather scientist can expect to earn anywhere from $50,000 to $130,000 annually, with an average salary of about $88,000.[8] There are a variety of careers possible for people interested in meteorology. An operational forecaster studies weather patterns and alerts the public to upcoming weather, while research scientists like Wurman focus on researching specific areas of weather.[9] Wurman is also the director of his own research center in Boulder, which he started in 1998. Its name is the Center for Severe Weather Research. He has a handful of employees and a small fleet of mobile radar units. He has used mobile radar units to study the winds in tornadoes, hurricanes, and wildfires across the United States and in Europe.

Wurman's center works closely with the National Center for Atmospheric Research. Much of the money for his research comes from the National Science

An inside look at a Doppler on Wheels.

Foundation, a federal agency that supports scientific research.

People in different careers support Wurman's research. For example, he works with an engineer who supplies weather equipment to scientists around the world, and he has worked with a filmmaker who made an IMAX film about tornadoes called *Tornado Alley*.

Wurman has also taught meteorology as a professor at the University of Oklahoma, University of Colorado, and Pennsylvania State University.[10]

Wurman says few scientists are as independent as he is, but he likes the freedom to pursue his own ideas. "I guess I have a very determined streak," he says.

Chapter 3

A Storm Lab in the Mountains

C an you imagine having a career in science where you strap on skis to get to the lab? That's just what Dr. Anna Gannet Hallar does. She is a weather scientist who is the director of the Storm Peak Laboratory. The laboratory sits atop Mt. Werner on the Steamboat Springs Ski Resort in Colorado. It is 10,500 feet (3,200 meters) above sea level, which is nearly 2 miles (3 kilometers) high.

During the summer, Hallar can drive up the mountain in an SUV or an all-terrain vehicle. In the winter, though, she generally uses skis and the resort's ski lifts to reach the lab.

"In the winter, I either drive or walk down to the ski resort and take the gondola [ski lift] to the top. Then, I have to ski down to catch another lift," she says.[1] She does this again to catch a third lift, which drops her off just a few feet from the lab.

The Storm Peak Lab overlooks a slope almost bare of trees. This long slope takes the brunt of every storm that hits the mountain. "We're extremely exposed, so we get pretty heavy storms," Hallar says. It gets windy, too. "It reached 100 miles [161 km] per hour [one] winter, and we were worried about losing instruments. We get struck by lightning frequently and lose power."

While lightning might knock out electrical power, Hallar says that the lab was designed to protect its occupants. "We're extremely well grounded. There are lightning rods all over the place."

Working in a mountaintop lab in the middle of a storm might not be everyone's idea of a dream job. Hallar finds the wild weather thrilling, though. "We had a cool storm," she said of a storm that happened one summer. "It was hailing and lightning, and the wind was shaking the windows. And then we came outside, and there was a double rainbow."

A Lofty Lab

The lab belongs to the Desert Research Institute (DRI) Division of Atmospheric Sciences (DAS). The DRI is a part of the Nevada System of Higher Education.[2] It has rooms for laboratory work. It also has a full kitchen and two bunkrooms, with enough beds for nine people. With this setup, scientists can work for days at a time, a group

A snowboarder makes his way down the slopes of the Steamboat ski area. Storm Peak Laboratory is located on top of Mount Werner in the Steamboat mountain range.

of students can make an overnight visit, and anyone caught by a storm can ride it out safely.

Both work and weather have kept Hallar in the lab overnight. "Some days we stay because we're studying the weather," she says. "[In winter] I'm normally working until it's dark and then skiing home in the dark, with headlamps. If it's blowing really hard, it isn't safe," because the blowing snow blocks the headlamps. When that is the case, she stays overnight. Her husband, Ian McCubbin, understands. He is also a scientist and the lab's associate research scientist.

The lab has electricity, but not all the comforts of home. Hallar and her husband make a weekly supply

Dr. Anna Gannet Hallar and her husband, Ian McCubbin, stand on the roof of the Storm Peak Lab.

A Special Laboratory

Storm Peak Laboratory is located on Mount Werner at the top of the Steamboat Springs Ski Resort in Colorado. Its elevation is 10,500 feet (3,200 meters) above sea level. It was built there so scientists could study the atmosphere above the turbulent layer near the ground. Storm Peak Laboratory is also a teaching facility for students from grade school through college. Special facilities include a full kitchen and bunks for nine people, a cold room for studying snow and ice, a rooftop deck where scientists take samples of air and clouds, and a computer lab.[3]

run. In the winter, that can mean hauling supplies up the mountain on a snowmobile towing a sled. They melt snow to make water for drinking, cooking, and washing.

The lab is there for the same reason Hallar is. Its lofty perch exposes it to free-flowing air that has not mixed with nearby surface-level dust and chemicals. This is a layer of the atmosphere that scientists call the free troposphere. The lab is also in clouds much of the time, which allows Hallar and others to study clouds without leaving the ground.

Measuring Air Pollution

Hallar's specialty is atmospheric chemistry, meaning she measures the chemicals in the air. Chemicals can range from the natural gases that make up the atmosphere to water droplets in clouds and airborne pollutants from human activities.

"I study mainly pollution and how atmospheric pollution affects humans," she says. Her research helps scientists understand how pollution made in one place can become a problem far away.

For example, as part of her ongoing research, she has taken air samples that were found to contain traces of mercury. Mercury is a metal that can cause serious health problems in humans. The burning of coal in power plants can release mercury into the air. Mercury can be a problem near where coal is burned, but Hallar was able to trace the mercury in her samples to eastern Asia. Her research showed that airborne mercury could drift halfway across the world.[4]

Becoming a Weather Scientist

Science has been a lifelong pursuit for Hallar, who admits she likes to tinker with scientific instruments. "I was definitely interested in science my whole life, but I got more interested in physics in high school. In college, I did an internship with the National Weather Service, and that was a life-changing event."

Hallar grew up on a farm in central Missouri and attended Truman State University in Kirksville, Missouri. During college, she received a summer internship at the National Weather Service's weather forecasting office in Pleasant Hill, Missouri. The internship offered college credit, as if she were taking a course. Better yet, it allowed

A view of Mount Werner in the Steamboat ski area.

Haller and her husband sometimes use a four-wheeler to drive back and forth from the lab.

her to sample different kinds of careers in weather science. "You got to do a little bit of everything," she recalls.

For example, as part of her internship she visited a local television station and watched a meteorologist work up the nightly weather report. She also took part in a program called SKY-WARN, which trains everyday people to become storm spotters for the National Weather Service. What impressed Hallar most was her visit to an automated weather station. It sparked her interest in the makeup of Earth's atmosphere.[5]

After earning a bachelor's degree in physics from Truman, Hallar went on to study atmospheric science in graduate school. She earned a master's degree from the University of Colorado at Boulder in 2001 and a PhD from that same university in 2003. In addition to her work in the field and the laboratory, Hallar is also currently an associate research professor for the Desert Research Institute in Reno, Nevada.

McMurdo Station, Antarctica

Hallar's studies led her all the way to Antarctica. In 2002, while she was still a graduate student, she flew in a US Air Force C-17 transport jet to McMurdo Station, the largest US outpost on the continent.[6] She studied the breakdown of ozone in the air. Ozone is a natural chemical in the

McMurdo Station is the largest research center in Antarctica. Hallar went there to study the ozone layer, which has been depleted over the years, particularly in Antarctica.

atmosphere that screens harmful ultraviolet rays from the Sun. Scientists have found that certain human-made chemicals in the air have weakened the ozone screen, especially over Antarctica.

Hallar was with a team of scientists studying how changes in sunlight affect ozone breakdown. The team arrived in August, at the tail end of the Antarctic winter when the days were still dark. "It's the coldest time of the year, actually. It was like minus 50[°F (−46°C)]," she says. They stayed until the Antarctic summer season, when there is daylight at all hours.

McMurdo might be the biggest outpost in Antarctica, but it is still small and remote. About one thousand people work there during the Antarctic summer, and the population dwindles to about 250 in winter. The station depends on ships and airplanes for supplies.[7]

"I was considered extremely lucky because I had a vehicle assigned to me," she says. "I had a car . . . because I had to go to a station outside of McMurdo, and I had to drive there." A typical McMurdo workday for Hallar started by bundling up in warm layers covered by a parka, driving on a rough road of volcanic rock to the research station, and then climbing onto its roof to melt ice off the weather instruments.

Sometimes she braved the cold just to escape the confines of McMurdo's cramped quarters. "You do need to get outside because you're there so long. I would take hikes and bundle up like crazy," she says.

A driller in Antarctica extracts a core of ice. Weather scientists can learn a great deal about the history of the earth's climate and weather from the ice in Antarctica.

Pollution in Paradise

What's the opposite of Antarctica? Perhaps it's the Maldives, a string of sunny coral islands in the Indian Ocean. Hallar went there in October 2004 as a research associate for the National Aeronautics and Space Administration (NASA). She went there to take part in an international study of air pollution.

The Maldives is far from any mainland, so it might be the last place you would think you could study air pollution, but Hallar found it there.

"It was a beautiful place and it was really nice," she says, but in October and November, air currents from India and Asia carry pollution across the northern islands. When that happens, she says, "[It's] like a smoggy day in Los Angeles. . . . It's kind of incredible."

Hallar's Maldives assignment came while she was working for NASA's Ames Research Center in northern California. She worked there from February 2004 to July 2006. NASA is known as America's space agency, but it also does a lot of research with airplanes. At Ames, Hallar worked on an instrument that was flown on NASA airplanes to study particles of pollution in the air. She didn't go on most flights, but it was her job to make sure the delicate instrument was working correctly. She also analyzed the data it collected.

Of the few research flights she has made, one during her college years stands out in her memory. In April 2000, when she was a graduate student at the University of Colorado, she flew on a C-130 transport plane. The

C-130 is a big plane with four propeller engines. The National Center for Atmospheric Research uses one for airborne research. Hallar went on a flight to study water vapor in the boundary layer. This is the layer of the atmosphere closest to Earth, and it can be bumpy. Hallar recalls climbing up to the cockpit for a pilot's-eye view of the flight. She enjoyed it, but when she climbed back down into the airplane's windowless cabin, the rocking and rolling motions made her sick. Since then, she has

Hallar traveled to the Maldives in the Indian Ocean to study air pollution.

been happy to let her instruments do the flying without her.

The Air Up There

At Storm Peak Lab, Hallar can study clouds and air pollution without leaving the ground or going halfway around the world. She described the lab in an interview with *Steamboat Today*, a local newspaper: "[The lab] allows us to do field research without having to travel. We can have a life. This is the perfect place," she said.[8]

Hallar also leads two National Science Foundation programs that support diversity. Geoscience Research at Storm Peak (GRASP) provides mentoring and field experiences to undergraduates. Atmospheric Science Collaborations and Enriching NeTworks (ASCENT) is a networking program for women in the atmospheric science field.[9]

Hallar enjoys her research. She says her favorite part of working in a scientific field is coming up with an idea about the atmosphere and then developing experiments to test her theory. "The results I find incredibly rewarding," she says. She also enjoys teaching schoolchildren who visit the lab and encouraging people from all backgrounds to enter scientific fields.

Chapter 4

Alaska's Wild Weather

Why would a weather scientist carry a gun? Dr. Gary Hufford brings a gun when he is working in the field in rural Alaska because he might need to protect himself from a grizzly bear. He is the senior scientist for the National Weather Service Alaska Region. Hufford's office is in the city of Anchorage, but his work often takes him out into remote areas, where bears and other wild animals are a common sight.[1]

"We're one of the few places where some of our [National Weather Service] employees are trained to handle a weapon," he says.[2]

Weather research in Alaska is a big job. Alaska is the biggest state in the union: It is more than twice the size of Texas. Alaska's jagged coastline, if it were stretched out

Dr. Gary Hufford conducts weather research in the Alaska region. His job involves a lot of travel in order to access remote areas of the state.

straight, could circle Earth twice. Its tallest mountain is nearly 4 miles (6 km) high.[3] It lies farther north than any other state, and it stretches across the Arctic Circle.

Roads reach only a small part of the huge state. "It means you do a lot of flying [to reach remote weather stations]," Hufford says. "Sometimes you have to go in by boat. To get to some of the sites, you have to do it in winter so you can land on skis on the snow. Other places you land on a local lake [in a plane equipped with floats] and hike over."

Getting to remote spots is not easy, nor is getting out of them. Hufford recalls a visit he made to a Weather Service station in McGrath, a town of a few hundred people in south central Alaska. He flew there in a small, single-engine airplane. While he was there, the temperature fell to −72°F (−58°C). The pilot would not try to start the plane—much less fly it—for fear that the deep cold would damage the engine. "The rule among [Alaskan] pilots is that they will not fly if it's colder than −40°F [−40°C]" Hufford says. When temperatures fall below that point, he says, an airplane's fuel can start turning to jelly, and if

In Alaska, float planes are used to land on lakes in the warmer months.

Reid Glacier in southeast Alaska is 11 miles (17 kilometers) long, but that could soon change as temperatures rise due to global warming.

an engine quits, it might not start again. Hufford had to wait six days until the severe cold eased.

Small Changes, Big Impact

It is easy to see why weather forecasting in Alaska is tricky, but something else might be making it even trickier: global warming.

Earth's surface has warmed by about one degree Fahrenheit (−17 degrees Celsius) over the past hundred years. The warming hasn't been the same everywhere, but on average the Arctic region has warmed almost twice as fast as other regions of the planet.[4]

Arctic areas like Alaska have been particularly hard hit by global warming. Frozen lakes like this one no longer stay frozen as long as they once might have.

Alaska is sensitive to climate change because much of it lies in a zone where a small change in temperature can have a big impact. "Unlike some places, where the difference between 74 degrees and 80 degrees [Fahrenheit (23–27°C)] may not mean much, two degrees here can cause great havoc," Hufford says. That is because temperatures across Alaska are often near the freezing point of water. A small change in temperature can mean the difference between frozen ground and mud, and between growing or shrinking sea ice along the coastline.

As temperatures have risen, Hufford has seen some big changes in Alaska's weather. For example, he says, bad

Global Warming

Global warming is the upward trend in the average temperature of Earth's surface. Scientists agree that Earth's surface has gradually warmed in recent centuries, and the rate of warming has increased. As Earth warms, glaciers and polar ice sheets have been melting, and the global average sea level has been rising.

In 2013 an international panel of scientists said that most of the global warming in the last half century was likely caused by humans—mainly from burning coal and oil, which puts carbon dioxide into the atmosphere. Carbon dioxide is what scientists call a greenhouse gas because it traps heat as a greenhouse does. The scientists predicted global warming will continue to get worse if people do not reduce activities that make greenhouse gases, such as burning coal and oil.[5]

storms on the Bering Sea are hitting the coastline more often. Ten storms socked the coast from 1980 to 1996. But a dozen storms hit in the following eight years. The storms caused flooding and washed away land. Some villages along the coast could be wiped out by another bad storm, Hufford says.

Is the rise in the number of storms caused by global warming? Is it a sign of things to come or just a short-term change? Hufford is trying to find out.

Forecasting the Future

"In the Weather Service, our main . . . mission is saving lives and property," Hufford says. Accurate forecasts can help people avoid or prepare for bad weather.

To forecast the weather for a certain place, a weather forecaster needs to know how weather usually behaves there. If you know how it behaves, you are better able to predict what it's likely to do next when it begins to change. How weather behaves from year to year in a certain place is called its climate. The study of climate is called climatology.

"Am I going to forecast 90 [°F (32°C)] tomorrow for Anchorage when it's 30 [°F (−1°C)] today? Climatology tells me I don't see those kinds of temperatures," Hufford says.

But that approach to predicting weather does not work if the climate is changing. Weather might start following new, unpredictable patterns. "If the climate is changing, then all of a sudden I'm going to start having [forecasting] problems," Hufford says. Hufford's research

A meteorologist in Alaska releases a weather balloon to collect information such as temperature, wind speed, and atmospheric pressure.

is aimed at learning how climate change affects short-term forecasts.

Hufford uses different methods to study Alaska's climate. For example, pictures from space satellites show him how much of the ocean off Alaska's coastline is covered with ice. It is important to know where the edge of the ice is. It can affect ocean traffic, fishing boats, and coastal villages whose residents venture out on the ice to hunt and fish.

To measure sea ice, Hufford created a system for catching almost any kind of satellite picture. This system is called the High Resolution Image Processing System, or HIPS. It grabs pictures radioed down from international satellites as they fly over Alaska. HIPS gives Hufford many satellite pictures that show the sea ice around Alaska.

Hufford says the satellite pictures show that Alaska's total area of sea ice has been shrinking at a rate of about 10 percent annually since the late 1970s. In addition, he has found that the sea ice also forms three weeks later in the year and melts three weeks sooner.

Sea Ice and Coastlines

It might sound like the changes in Alaska's climate are small and slow, but Hufford says they have a great impact on people who live near the ocean. That's because the sea ice helps protect the coastline from damage caused by storms. "Sea ice acts like an extension of land. People living along the coast are no more affected [by storms]

The Impact of Climate Change in Alaska

Global warming is behind many problems faced by the state of Alaska. These woes include melting glaciers, rising sea levels, and flooding of coastal communities. The warming of oceans and the melting of land-based ice increases the volume of ocean water. The loss of sea ice cover alters the habitats of Arctic species and leaves coastal communities more exposed to larger waves generated by severe storms. Because of these changes, more than 160 Alaskan coastal villages are threatened by coastline erosion. Three—Shishmaref, Kivalina, and Newtok—have plans in place for relocating inland, but the cost of doing so is disheartening. Thawing permafrost—or ground that used to stay frozen year round—and more violent storms are damaging roads, utilities, pipelines, and buildings. Rising sea levels and changes in rain and snowfall will affect safe water sources in villages, contribute to the erosion of coastlines and riverbeds, and damage Alaska's vast forests.

Changes that affect wildlife hurt native Alaskans' way of life, which depends on hunting and fishing. For example, the loss of coastal sea ice makes traditional hunting and fishing on the ice more difficult and dangerous. Alaska also has witnessed a record loss of forests to fires and spruce bark beetles, which have spread as the climate has warmed.[6]

than if they lived inland. Without sea ice, storms build bigger waves, causing coastal flooding."

Combine the loss of sea ice with more frequent storms, and the impact of climate change becomes even more severe. Because of the flooding, the people of some coastal villages are trying to move their communities to new locations.[7]

Satellite data helps scientists like Hufford measure climate change. But the kind of satellite data that Hufford uses has only been available since the 1970s. Even weather data taken on the ground in Alaska covers a relatively small range of years. However, to get a truly

Global warming is causing glaciers to melt and form lakes like this one.

The weather services uses remote weather stations like the one shown here to track the weather across Alaska. Tracking weather helps scientists to learn more about climate change.

accurate measure of a region's climate, scientists need to know the average of its weather over many decades. "That's a real challenge [in Alaska], because we're a young state," Hufford says. For example, he says regular weather observations for Anchorage did not begin until around 1920. That is a short time for gathering data on the climate. "We simply don't have those long-term records that you find in other places."

Year by year, the Weather Service is building those records. It uses a network of small, ground-based weather stations with automated instruments to observe the weather across Alaska. It also has larger stations with weather observers scattered across the state. Part of Hufford's job is to find good spots for new weather stations and to periodically check the stations.

Bears: A Job Hazard

Hufford says he does not go out into the field alone because of the risk of bear attacks. Bears are less likely to attack a pair of people, and they are much less likely to attack a group of three, he says.

Some bears have put this idea to the test. Hufford was leading a group of three people at Cold Bay on the Alaskan Peninsula, where they were checking the site to see if it would be a good location for a weather station.

"We were out on Russell Creek. This is the only major salmon stream for many miles around. For that reason, it is not unusual to see half a dozen to a dozen brown bears fishing on any given day."

The scientists were studying the site and "not paying too much attention," Hufford admits, when a mother bear and two cubs burst out of the bushes along the creek just a few dozen yards away. "This was too close an encounter, and she charged."

Hufford was sure the bears were going to attack. "But as she charged us with her cubs, she got within about 30 feet [9 meters], and she simply stopped and broke off and took off in another direction.

"Her cubs were so tied up on us—they're still staring at us. They slow up a little bit, turn to look where Mom is, and Mom is gone. This is in June, and what was happening was [the mother bear] was dumping her cubs on us."

Hufford says the cubs were old enough to be on their own. He thinks their mother was looking for a chance to get away. "She wanted to get their attention on us while she took off."

Hufford's group froze, and waited to see if the cubs would keep charging. The group was armed with a rifle and a handgun, but they did not want to shoot unless they had to.

"As soon as they realized Mom was gone, [the cubs] came to a total stop," Hufford says. "They spent two or three minutes wandering around trying to figure out what to do, then took off."

Spending time in the wilderness of Alaska means that it is not unusual for Hufford to spot bears as he works.

A Career in the Outdoors

The outdoors was always a part of Hufford's life. He grew up along the McKenzie River near Eugene, Oregon. His father was a boat guide there, who took people on fishing trips. Those trips sparked Hufford's curiosity about water and weather. "I was real curious about the environment. When I got into high school, I had a teacher who was very influential who really encouraged me to go towards science."

His curiosity about rivers and other waterways steered Hufford towards oceanography—the study of the oceans. But then he also became interested in what happens where ocean and air meet. For example, heat and moisture from the ocean feed hurricanes. While studying oceanography, Hufford says, "I took so many meteorology courses, I qualified for a meteorologist." He earned a bachelor's degree in general science from Oregon State University in 1964 and a master's degree in oceanography in 1967. He earned a PhD in oceanography from the University of Connecticut in 1978.

Hufford came to Alaska to do field research and complete his doctorate and has lived there ever since. Working for the National Weather Service means that he is an employee of the federal government. The government's 2015 salary range for his position and level of seniority is $91,000 to $108,000. This salary range reflects a locality payment of 25 percent higher than in other parts of the country because living expenses are higher than the national average in Alaska.[8] Hufford loves living in Alaska because he loves the outdoors. When he is not on the job, Hufford co-owns a fishing lodge and is a part-time fishing guide.

Chapter 5

Into the Eye of a Hurricane

Most people flee inland to escape the flooding and winds that hurricanes bring when they barrel toward the coastline. Weather scientists sometimes do just the opposite. Dr. Wen-Chau Lee has flown through two of history's most destructive hurricanes. It was all in the name of science, because he was collecting data that will help scientists better understand how these intense storms work.

Lee is a senior scientist with the National Center for Atmospheric Research in Boulder, Colorado. He focuses his research on hurricanes, and specializes in using airborne Doppler radars to observe winds inside hurricanes.

People have known and feared hurricanes for centuries. Modern weather forecasters track them with

Dr. Wen-Chau Lee studies hurricanes using airborne Doppler radar.

airplanes and satellites. But much about hurricanes remains a mystery, Lee says. "We know the hurricane structure very well, especially in the mature stage. However, we still don't understand why and how it forms in the clouds organize to form a vortex is unknown, not clear."

By flying an airplane into a hurricane, scientists can measure the speed, direction, temperature, pressure, and humidity of the storm's swirling winds. But Lee says that doing this gives data only from along the line the plane flies through the storm. To get a better sense of what hurricanes are like, scientists blend data from many flights through many hurricanes.

That, too, provides an incomplete picture, Lee says. "It smooths the features out so you can get an idea of what hurricanes look like, but you cannot tell the character of an individual hurricane." He compares it to taking a person's picture with a low quality digital camera. "You can sort of figure out that's a person, but you can hardly tell what that person looks like."

Lee is trying to sharpen our view of hurricanes. He uses Doppler radar to see into the heart of the storm. He says it's like using x-rays to see inside a human body, although the Doppler radar uses radio waves instead of x-rays. "The radar can probe the internal structure of a hurricane," Lee says.

NOAA scientists like Lee often use P-3 Orion aircraft like this one to study hurricanes.

A Closer Look

Getting a good look at a hurricane is hard to do. Hurricanes usually form over the open ocean, far from land and ground-based radars. Some newer satellites use radio waves to probe hurricanes. But satellites are thousands of miles up in space, and they do not have powerful radars. Again, Lee compares them to a digital camera that takes fuzzy pictures. That is not all: In the past, it took two radars probing the same hurricane from different angles to get good measurements.

Lee solves both problems by taking radar units close to hurricanes in an airplane. In fact, the plane flies right into them!

Airplanes have been used to study hurricanes for many years. The Air Force Reserve's Hurricane Hunters squadron flies through hurricanes to measure and track them. The National Oceanic and Atmospheric Administration (NOAA) flies two airplanes through hurricanes to study them. These airplanes are Lockheed P-3 Orions. The Orion is the size of a small airliner. It has four propellers. It also has special equipment to gather data about a hurricane. In the tail of each plane is a Doppler radar. About fifteen people fly in an Orion on a hurricane mission. Lee has flown on several missions in the NOAA planes to probe hurricanes with radar.

Lee's first hurricane flight was in 1995. He was studying Hurricane Luis over the Atlantic Ocean. He remembers it well because it was a night flight. Both of the Orion planes were in the hurricane. They were flying in patterns that sliced through the center of the powerful storm. Around the eye, or the center of the storm, the circling winds had formed a tight wall of clouds called the eyewall. The eye itself was clear.

"The first time we entered the eye it was near midnight and there was a full moon," Lee recalls. The winds in the eyewall were strong but smooth, and the air in the eye itself was calm. "I remember the captain said, 'Okay, you guys have about five minutes to walk around before we reach the eyewall on the other side.'"

Lee took off his seat belt and went to a window. "I saw this beautiful full moon, and I could see a very pale color like silver on the inside of the eye. There were two aircraft in the storm, both NOAA P-3s, so I knew at that time there were thirty people in there. No one else."

Weather scientists do not fly the airplane on a hurricane research flight. Each P-3 has two professional pilots who control the plane. Although Lee doesn't fly the plane, he says it's a scientist's job to lead the mission and tell the pilots where to fly. They do this to tell the pilot how to avoid the most dangerous weather while still enabling the scientists to collect good data.

Lee flew on two missions into Hurricane Luis. Surprisingly, he says he didn't bounce around too badly. In part, he says, that's because the more powerful hurricanes tend to have smoother winds. But it is also because the scientist leading the mission was watching the screens of two radars: one in the tail that is used to collect data and one in the nose that is used to look

More About Hurricanes

- The word *hurricane* comes from "Hurican," which was the name of a mythical Caribbean god of evil.

- A tropical storm becomes known as a hurricane when its winds reach 74 miles (119 km) per hour. Some hurricanes have had winds of nearly 200 miles (322 km) per hour!

- Hurricanes get their strength from warm ocean waters. Evaporation from seawater increases the storm's power.

- Hurricanes are dangerous because they can bring high winds, heavy rainfall, and large waves called storm surges.

- As hurricanes move inland away from the ocean, they lose their source of energy and die.

- Hurricane season is the time of the year when hurricanes are most likely to form. It is from June 1 through November 30.

- Typhoons are the same as hurricanes, except they happen in the western Pacific Ocean.[1]

ahead for dangerous turbulence. Lee says part of the lead scientist's job is to warn the pilots of rough air ahead so they can dodge it.

Lee did not lead the missions into Hurricane Luis, or the mission he flew into Hurricane Jeanne in 2004. "In these two hurricanes, my role was pretty much a passenger, an instrument operator. I did not have the

Hurricane Luis slammed into the Caribbean island of St. Martin in September 2007. Here, boats lay on the shore in the aftermath of the storm.

responsibility to guide the aircraft," he says. Part of his job was to learn what hurricane flights were like so he could lead them later.

That happened in 2005, when Lee found himself guiding a P-3 Orion through two of the most dangerous storms ever to hit the United States: Hurricane Katrina and Hurricane Rita.

Intense Storms

Scientists rate a hurricane's strength on a scale of one to five. Five is the strongest. A hurricane becomes a Category 5 storm when its winds reach 156 miles (251 km) per hour. It changes categories as it grows stronger or weaker. Katrina and Rita both reached Category 5 at their peaks.

Katrina formed in late August of 2005 and swept across south Florida before growing into a Category 5 storm over the Gulf of Mexico. Its winds weakened before it struck the coasts of Louisiana and Mississippi. It drove ashore huge waves called a storm surge. It battered and flooded communities along the coast. Most media attention focused on flooded parts of New Orleans, Louisiana, but other towns also saw severe damage. Katrina ultimately caused $108 billion in damage, making it the costliest natural disaster in history of the United States.[2]

Rita followed in less than a month. After peaking at Category 5, it came ashore at the Texas–Louisiana border as a Category 3 storm. More than three million people fled from its path. While powerful, Rita caused far less death and destruction than Katrina.[3]

It was the first time in recorded history that the Gulf of Mexico saw two Category 5 hurricanes in the same season. And the hurricane doubleheader came at a time when several US laboratories were making a big effort to study the inner workings of hurricanes.

What the scientists wanted to study were the storm's eyewall—where a hurricane's winds are the fastest— and its rain bands. Rain bands are bands of heavy rain and wind that spiral outward from the storm's center. Scientists wanted to learn how the eyewall and the rain bands affected each other to change a storm's intensity.

Hurricane Katrina, seen here from space, was the third deadliest storm in the history of the United States.

Into the Storm

For Katrina and Rita, three Orion planes would fly through the hurricanes: NOAA's two P-3s and a Navy P-3 that carried a more powerful Doppler radar. Lee led the Navy plane's missions.

"I had to tell the pilot where to fly. That was quite a nerve-wracking experience," Lee recalls. "You really do not enjoy these flights. You are responsible not only for the [flight's] scientific success, but you're also responsible for the safety of the crew. If you tell the pilot to make the wrong turn, the outcome can be pretty bad."

Lee says the idea was to fly between the rain bands and probe them with the radar—but to avoid the bands themselves. The rain and wind between the bands were bad enough, but inside them the storm could be dangerously rough. During the flights, Lee kept an eye on the nose radar's screen to watch for dangerous weather in their path. Sometimes he would have to tell the pilot to swerve around a dangerous patch of sky. "That [was] a very intense operation," he says.

No matter what, flying inside a hurricane isn't a smooth ride. Lee's airplane plowed through some rain bands to reach the parts of the storm where the team wanted to collect data. Lee says the airplane shook and lurched through updrafts and downdrafts, and the din of the storm came through the cabin walls. "You can hear the rain pounding on the fuselage [the airplane's body]. And occasionally when we penetrate the rain band or the eyewall, there is some large hail. You hear the ice [hitting] the fuselage." As turbulent as it was, Lee said he never got airsick. "Each person's tolerance is different," he says.

But the missions were exciting because the radar on Lee's plane could see five times more detail than the radars on the other planes. Lee likens it to switching to a better camera to take someone's picture. "You suddenly

! Categorizing Hurricanes

The National Hurricane Center measures hurricane intensity using a scale called the Saffir-Simpson Hurricane Scale. A storm becomes a Category 1 hurricane when its winds reach 74 to 95 miles per hour (119–153 km/h). From 96 to 110 mph (154–177 km/h), it is a Category 2 storm. Category 3 ranges from 111 to 129 mph (178–208 km/h). Category 4 storms have winds from 130 to 156 mph (209–251 km/h), and storms with higher winds are Category 5—the highest category.

see a lot of detail of this person's face. . . . You start to see the eyes, the nose, the lips," he says.

The radar showed new details of eyewalls forming and changing. Lee's plane's radar caught two eyewalls in Rita—the one surrounding the eye and a new one that had formed from rain bands outside the inner eyewall. Scientists believe rain bands in a hurricane tighten to form a new eyewall, which chokes off and replaces the

A NOAA High Altitude Sampling jet flies near Hurricane Katrina in the Florida Keys as the co-pilot studies recent satellite images of the storm.

inner one. They call this process the eyewall replacement cycle. "Typically when the hurricane goes through this type of cycle, it intensifies. That's why we're so interested in capturing this process," Lee says.

Lee said that the research adds to what we know about hurricanes and helps NOAA's National Hurricane Center make better forecasts. Forecasting what a hurricane will do before it strikes land can save many lives.

Lee says that it's rewarding to see his research make a difference in forecasting. "When other scientists start to use your work . . . you know every time there's a hurricane your work is involved and affects the prediction that the hurricane center's making. That's quite satisfactory."

America's Deadliest Hurricanes

The deadliest hurricane to hit the United States was an unnamed storm that struck Galveston, Texas, in 1900. It killed about eight thousand people. The high number of fatalities caused by this storm were probably the result of numerous factors such as lack of tracking technology and Galveston's vulnerable position along the Gulf of Mexico.

An unnamed storm struck southeastern Florida in 1920, and killed 2,500. Hurricane Katrina was the third deadliest storm in US history. This 2005 storm was blamed for 1,500 deaths.[4]

Making a Difference

Wen-Chau Lee was born in Taiwan, an island of East Asia. He remembers two books his father gave him when he was young. One was about weather, and the other was about insects. "I ended up looking at the weather book much, much more than I looked at the insect book," he says.

No wonder. Taiwan is less than three hundred miles long, but typhoons—the western Pacific version of hurricanes—hit it an average of 3.5 times per year, Lee says. "There's no shortage of weather there, so that just fascinated me."

He wanted to study atmospheric science in college, but his parents wanted him to study engineering. Lee says he listed engineering for both of his top two choices of course study when he applied for college. He listed atmospheric science third. Lee then took Taiwan's tough college entrance test, which is similar to tests US students take before entering college. After taking the entrance test Lee was given his third choice. He earned a bachelor of science degree in atmospheric science from National Taiwan University in 1981.

Rescuers in a boat help local residents who are trapped after a typhoon in Taiwan. Lee was inspired by the typhoons in his home country to pursue extreme weather as a career.

After his undergraduate studies, Lee came to the United States to continue his education. In 1985, he completed a master's degree at the University of California in Los Angeles and in 1988 he attained his doctorate there, too. In his graduate studies, he focused his research on the use of Doppler radar for severe weather observation. He says he specialized in hurricanes because he thought he might return to Taiwan to teach and he could apply that knowledge to teaching about typhoons. However, Lee says, he stayed in the United States because it offered the best atmospheric research programs and facilities—and "the best opportunity for a young scientist to make a difference."

Unlocking Lightning's Mysteries

Dr. Earle Williams knows that thunderstorms can be a hair-raising experience. Sometimes the experience is *literally* hair-raising!

Williams is a senior research scientist at the renowned Massachusetts Institute of Technology (MIT) in Cambridge. His specialty is lightning. This field of study has taken Williams all around the world to observe thunderstorms. His most vivid memory of a storm happened while he was on vacation, though. He was visiting the Grand Canyon, when he noticed a storm cloud building over the canyon. He then watched as a tourist group taking photos at a railing along the rim of the canyon.

"They were all snapping pictures of one another. . . . When you looked closely, you'd see their hair stand

Lightning strikes through a cloudburst over the Grand Canyon.

up suddenly and then relax, and stand up and relax," Williams recalls.[1] The tourists were getting a "charge" out of the gathering storm. An electrostatic charge, to be precise. It is just like the static charge that might shock you after you rub your feet on a rug, but on a much bigger and more dangerous scale.

The storm cloud was building up powerful electrostatic charges. The base of the storm held a negative charge, and it was teasing up a positive charge in the ground below—and in the people who were standing on the ground.[2]

"The electrostatic field was influencing their hair, but they didn't know what was going on. They were just amused and taking pictures of one another," he recalls.

What the tourists didn't know, however, was that they were close to becoming human lightning rods! Opposite electrical charges attract, and the positive charge in the ground was trying to join the negative charge in the sky. All that kept them apart was the air. If the charge in the cloud built up enough, it would overcome the gap like a giant spark plug. The result could be a sudden flash of lightning as the cloud discharged electrons to the ground—and possibly right through the people!

"That's the kind of situation that is very dangerous, because you know there is a big [electrostatic] field in the ground. There's plenty of energy to carry the lightning from the cloud to the ground and kill somebody," Williams says.

Despite the danger, Williams says he walked down to the group to warn them. He discovered they were Japanese tourists who did not speak English. They could not understand him. They were lucky; the storm hurled no lightning.

A Dazzling Light Show

A thunderstorm is nature's most dazzling light show. One of the great mysteries of weather is how clouds build up the electricity to make lightning. Both are reasons why scientists like Williams study lightning.

Dr. Earle Williams studies how the electricity in lightning is formed during a thunderstorm.

What Is Lightning?

A thunderstorm starts to form when moist, unstable air near the ground is forced to rise. This can happen when the sun-warmed ground heats the air above it, starting an updraft. It can also happen when an approaching cold front forces warmer air to rise. As the air rises, it loses heat. The moisture in the air then condenses, forming a tall cloud. Some of the moisture falls out as rain, causing a downdraft. Other moisture freezes to the surface of small airborne particles. This forms ice crystals, larger ice particles called graupel, and hail.

The ice particles ride in the updrafts and downdrafts, colliding and building up static electricity (electrons) in the storm cloud. The top of the cloud becomes positively charged, and the base of the cloud becomes negatively charged.

If the charges become great enough, electrons will leap across the gap to other clouds or to the ground, causing a lightning flash.

The lightning superheats the air around it, causing it to expand with a boom of thunder.[3]

There are more down-to-earth reasons, too. Lightning kills people and sparks forest fires. And it can strike in strange ways.

You might think the safest place to be in a thunderstorm is deep underground. But lightning, according to a federal government report, likely caused a deadly coal-mine disaster in West Virginia. Twelve miners died in the Sago Mine after a pocket of methane gas exploded on January 2, 2006. It caved in the mine entrance and filled the tunnels with deadly fumes. Investigators believe a lightning strike on the surface sent an electric jolt through a cable that went into the mine, triggering a spark that ignited the gas.[4]

The odds that you will ever be hit by lightning are only one in five thousand, according to the National Weather Service. Still, lightning kills an average of sixty-two people every year in the United States—that's about as many as tornadoes kill.[5] Williams says better warnings could lower lightning's death toll, but better warnings depend on a deeper understanding of how thunderstorms work.

Williams has studied lightning around the world, especially on land near the equator. He says tropical areas are the best breeding grounds for thunderstorms because they get warmer than other parts of Earth— much warmer than an ocean surface, which is why more thunderstorms form over land. The hot ground warms the air above it and creates strong updrafts, a key ingredient in thunderstorms. The top three thunderstorm regions in the world are equatorial Africa, South America, and an area of the western Pacific Ocean around Indonesia. Williams says the big thunderstorms in the Midwestern United States match any in the world, but scientists study storms in the tropics because they can count on seeing one nearly every day.

Inside a Faraday Cage

Studying lightning can be dangerous work, but Williams says there are ways to work safely. "I know lots of people who study lightning, but I've never heard of an injury or a hazard to anyone who's keenly interested in lightning," he says. "They know how to protect themselves."

Williams led a lightning research expedition to western Africa in 2006. The team set up a research station on flat desert land in Niger. They shipped their gear in trailer-sized metal shipping containers. The containers

Dr. Earle Williams and his daughter, Allegra, pose together while hunting thunderstorms in Niger, Africa.

Allegra Williams uses a very sensitive light detection device that can detect the flash from a lightning strike 30 miles (48 kilometers) away during the middle of the day. This is used to measure the average flash rate of a storm.

were then used as their research quarters. Williams says they made excellent lightning shelters. Any lightning that hit them would be conducted to the ground on the outer surface of the metal. Says Williams, "Every facility I've worked in is basically a metal enclosure of some sort, which is very good protection against lightning."

Metal enclosures made especially for this purpose are called Faraday cages. They are named after British physicist Michael Faraday, who was a pioneer in the understanding of electricity. Williams says a metal car can act as a Faraday cage to protect its occupants in an electrical storm. But a car is not a perfect enclosure, as he has experienced firsthand.

"I remember one time driving along a highway in Orlando, Florida, in a big thunderstorm. There was a lightning flash to a road marker just to the left of my vehicle, probably within three feet [one meter] of me. And I could feel it. . . . I could feel the electrostatic effects." Williams says the window in the car door had a big enough gap for a bit of the charge to reach him. "That's an example of having a Faraday cage with a hole in it."

That was not his only close encounter with lightning. Interestingly, none of his close encounters have occurred while he was actually studying lightning. Williams says

Cars and other vehicles are generally a safe place to be when lightning strikes. It is the car's steel frame, and not the tires, that protects occupants from the lightning.

his only close brush on a research trip came while he was taking a break from his work.

That happened on a research project in northern Australia near Darwin. Williams's family accompanied him on the trip, and he took them sightseeing one weekend. Along came what Williams calls a "runaway thunderstorm." It got that name because during this kind of thunderstorm the lightning flashes nonstop. "This one was a very spectacular one, and the storm came right overhead, and the lightning hit a TV mast and blew sparks all over the place. . . . That one really got my attention."

Earth's Global Circuit

Williams does some of his worldwide research without leaving the United States. He can monitor thunderstorms around the world from a single station in Rhode Island. Its main instrument is a big metal ball on a pole.

Earth has what is called a global circuit. That means that the upper atmosphere carries a positive charge, while Earth's surface has a negative charge. The gap between those charged layers forms the waveguide, which is a zone in which a pulse of electromagnetic energy sends waves of a certain frequency all the way around the planet.

When a thunderstorm fires up somewhere on Earth, each lightning flash sends out these waves. A strong storm with lots of flashes generates waves strong enough to be detected by the instrument in Rhode Island. The

Lightning strikes over New York's Empire State Building in July 2014.

A long line of well-organized thunderstorm cells approach the MIT radar run by Dr. Williams in Niamey, Niger.

instrument allows scientists like Williams to measure daily thunderstorm activity around the planet.

Williams says that studying the daily thunderstorm activity around the world might reveal clues to global climate change. He said he began thinking about the link on his trips to the tropics. In observing the lightning closely, he noticed that when the temperature rose slightly, there was more lightning. When the temperature dropped, so did the lightning activity, Williams wonders whether the entire planet will respond in the same way as smaller regions do. Will a warmer Earth mean more lightning-producing storms?

Lightning Facts

- The United States sees about twenty-five million lightning flashes each year.

- Lightning has caused an average of twenty-six deaths per year between 2010 and 2014. An average of three hundred lightning-related injuries are reported each year, but the National Weather Service thinks some cases go unreported, so the actual number is likely higher.[6]

- Lightning can strike as far as 10 miles (16 km) from where it is raining. That is about how far the sound of thunder travels. If you can hear thunder, you are within striking distance of lightning. Seek safe shelter immediately.

- Most lightning deaths and injuries occur in the summer. The National Weather Service urges that outdoor sport activities should stop at the first roar of thunder to give everyone time to get into a large building or enclosed vehicle.

- If you are indoors during a storm, do not use corded telephones, computers, or other devices with electrical cords. Stay away from pools, tubs, showers, and other plumbing.

- Wait thirty minutes after the last clap of thunder before going outdoors again.[7]

Williams first became interested in storms as a child, but it was studying science in college that sparked his curiosity about lightning and led to his career as a severe-storm scientist.

Williams says scientists do not yet know how global warming affects thunderstorm activity worldwide. But keeping track of thunderstorms worldwide over many years will help scientists learn more about both global warming and thunderstorms.

A Lifelong Passion

Williams thinks that where he lived when he was young had a lot to do with his interest in thunderstorms. He was born in South Bend, Indiana, and lived for 20 years in Culver, Indiana, about 40 miles (64 kilometers) from

South Bend. "There are great storms coming through there, really blockbusters," he says.

His father was also a big influence on his passion for science. "He was an artist, a sculptor, but he was also a telescope maker, and he had a broad range of [scientific] interests."

In college, Williams did not set out to study lightning. He studied physics and electromagnetic energy, which led to a fascination with the physics of lightning. "It was really lightning that drew me into studying storms," he says. "Once I was interested in lightning, I needed to learn meteorology." Studying meteorology helped him understand how thunderstorms work.

Williams earned a bachelor's degree in physics from Swarthmore College in Swarthmore, Pennsylvania, in 1974. He earned a PhD in geophysics from MIT in 1981. Williams says that a weather scientist with his credentials may earn between $106,000 and $178,000.[8] Where a person's salary falls within that range depends on whether he or she chooses to teach. He says that it is possible to earn more by working as a scientist for a private company. "But then you lose the freedom to do what you want to do," he says.

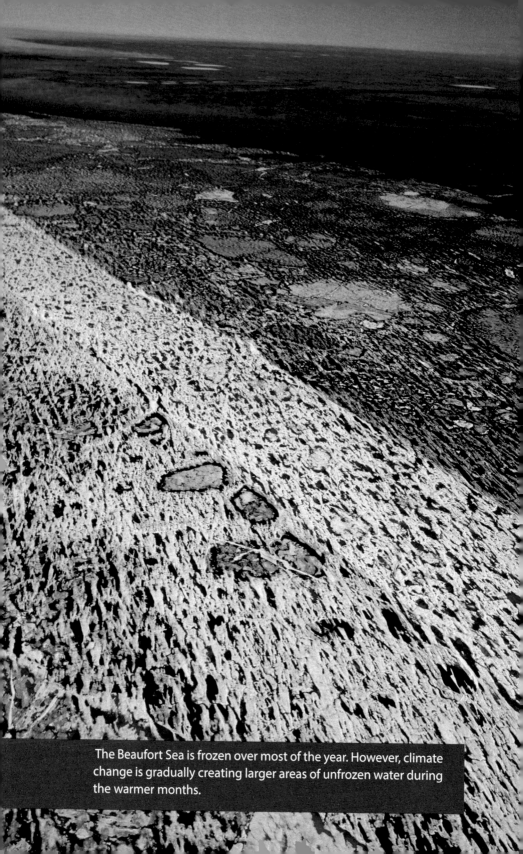

The Beaufort Sea is frozen over most of the year. However, climate change is gradually creating larger areas of unfrozen water during the warmer months.

Chapter 7

Climate Clues in Sea Ice

The Beaufort Sea is part of the Arctic Ocean. It stretches from Alaska and Canada's Northwest Territories to the North Pole. Much of the Beaufort Sea is covered in ice throughout the year. Winters there are dark and frigid, and even the long summer days can have snow or freezing rain. The sea is frequented by whales, seals, and polar bears—and by scientists like Dr. Jennifer Hutchings.

Hutchings is a British physicist who is an assistant professor at Oregon State University in Corvallis. She teaches the physics of oceans and atmospheres. Prior to that, she was a physicist at the University of Alaska in Fairbanks, where she worked at the International Arctic Research Center. Her research specialty throughout her career has been sea ice. Like many other scientists, she

The animals that live in the Arctic Ocean, like this ringed seal pup, are seeing their habitats shrink as Earth's surface warms.

uses high-tech tools in her work. For example, data from space satellites helps her gauge the extent and thickness of sea ice. But satellites cannot tell her everything. To understand sea ice, she needs to go out on the ice itself. For several years, she did just that, sometimes twice a year. It is hard, dangerous work.[1]

Scientists have been paying close attention to Arctic sea ice. Ice covers much of the Arctic Ocean year round in a great mass called an ice pack. At its winter peak, it covers some six million square miles (15,540,000 km^2). That's an area nearly twice the size of the United States! But more of the sea ice has been melting in the summer. Scientists have noticed the ice beginning to melt earlier in the year and forming later.[2]

The Arctic Ocean's shrinking ice pack is one of many clues scientists have found that Earth's surface is getting warmer. But sea ice is not as simple a thing as ice on a lake. It is a vast mass of frozen water that lies between the ocean and the air, so sea ice affects how heat moves from one to the other. It even has an impact on how heat circulates through the world's oceans. Its annual cycle of forming and melting plays a complex role in Earth's climate. It is a role scientists are trying hard to understand.[3]

Ice on the Move

In winter, the Arctic ice pack is so massive that it looks like another continent. It is so vast, that it gives no hint

95

What Is Sea Ice?

Sea ice is frozen ocean water. It freezes and melts in the ocean. Although it is not made of snow, it usually becomes covered with snow.

More sea ice remains through summer in the Arctic than in the Antarctic. A major reason for this is that land nearly surrounds the Arctic Ocean, so the ice cannot easily drift off to other oceans and melt. Arctic sea ice also tends to become trapped in a swirling pattern of surface water called the Beaufort Gyre. Ice floes drifting in the gyre may stay frozen for several years and bump into other floes, forming thick pack ice.

The year-round Arctic ice pack has been measured at around two million square miles (5,180,000 km²). At the end of winter, the ice pack covers about six million square miles (15,540,000 km²). As huge as the Arctic ice pack is, scientists say more of it melts every summer because of global warming; if the trend continues, they say, summers on the Arctic Ocean could become ice-free. [4]

that it is floating. "You really feel like you're on solid ground," says Hutchings.

But the ice pack is not solid. Tides, ocean currents, and storms push the sea ice around. Hutchings says the ice pack is a collection of huge pieces of sea ice that are constantly smashing together, grinding, and cracking. A crack can split the ice for miles, exposing stretches of open water called leads. The exposed water gives up heat to the air and forms new ice. If the lead stays open, the

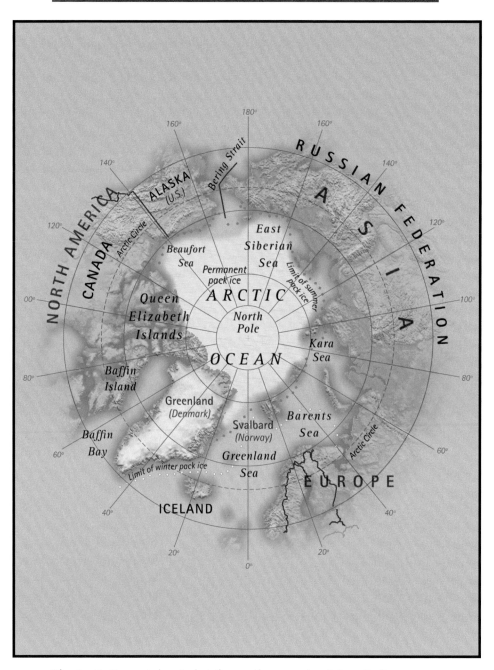

The Arctic Ocean is located at the northernmost point on Earth.

Dr. Jennifer Hutchings specializes in sea ice.

new ice will thicken. If it closes, it will crumple the new ice into jagged ridges. The ridges may be several yards high and dozens of yards deep. All of this affects how much ice forms and how much of it lasts through the summer.

Hutchings focuses her research on the forces that move and reshape sea ice. She wants to understand how those forces affect ice formation. She uses her knowledge in working with other scientists to develop computer programs to predict changes in the Arctic ice pack. She hopes her research will improve our understanding of Earth's climate and the forces that affect it.

Studying sea ice is difficult and expensive. The Beaufort Sea is remote, and conditions are harsh. Research projects are usually joint efforts of government agencies and universities. Many projects involve more than one country.

Hutchings likes to go out on the Beaufort ice at the end of winter, when the ice pack is at its peak, and at the end of summer, when it is at its lowest point. "[These are] the two periods when you can [best] compare the ice," she says.

Icebreakers

Hutchings's summer visits are generally between late July and early September. She travels to the ice on an icebreaker. An icebreaker is a powerful ship with a strong hull built for smashing through ice. The icebreaker is almost always on the move, so Hutchings sees much more sea ice on these cruises than she does at the winter ice camps. The Arctic summer has twenty-four hours of daylight, so scientists are able to work around the clock.

What is the weather like on a summer Arctic cruise? "It feels like winter because the ice is everywhere and it's cold. But from my perspective, being there in the summer is rather nice," Hutchings says. That's because it is far warmer than in winter, when she visits the ice camps. On the summer cruises, "You don't have to worry about how many layers of gloves you want to wear

An icebreaker is a ship with a strong hull for smashing through ice. On the ice, Hutchings and her colleagues are taking and testing samples.

and how you're going to write in your notebook when [the wind is blowing] outside." But it is often foggy, she says. That is because the ocean releases moisture into the chilly air. The moisture quickly condenses into clouds of tiny water droplets, forming a fog that can blanket the sea.

In summer, the southern Beaufort Sea looks like a jigsaw puzzle coming apart as the ice pack breaks up. The broken-up ice pieces are called floes. The icebreaker can either weave between the floes or smash through them. Sometimes it stops at a floe so scientists can set up a station to study it more closely.

Ice floes like those seen here are the result of climate change. Hutchings and her team study ice formations to better understand the forces that affect our climate.

THREE RIVERS PUBLIC LIBRARY

Hutchings enjoys these stops. "I love being out on the ice. It's so special. It's a different world. It's almost like being on the moon sometimes, because it's so alien. It's a very peaceful environment," she says. It's a big contrast from the ship. "The ship is noisy all the time."

In the summer of 2007, Hutchings traveled on the Canadian Coast Guard icebreaker *Louis S. St-Laurent*. The ship carried fifty-one crewmembers; twenty-seven scientists from the United States, Canada, and Japan; and a Japanese news team.[5] Most of the scientists were working on a project to study the water in the Beaufort Sea. But Hutchings and one of her students, Alice Orlich, were on the cruise to study the ice. The two worked in shifts; while one slept, the other made hourly observations of the thickness and condition of the pack ice.

The View From Above

The *Louis S. St-Laurent* cruise was an especially exciting one for Hutchings. She flew over the sea in a helicopter launched from the ship. The ship uses the helicopter to scout the easiest path through the floes. The scientists use it to scout for good places to set up ice stations. Hutchings flew along as an ice station scout. The flights also gave her a bird's eye view of the ice she was studying.

The back of the ship has a landing deck for the helicopter. "It's quite exciting actually, taking off and landing from the ship," Hutchings says.

Hutchings says her flights ranged up to a 100 miles (160 km) from the ship. Flying over an icy ocean, far from ship and shore, can be dangerous. Before flying, she took a survival course to learn how to get out of the helicopter if it went into the ocean.

"We dress warm, and we wear a life jacket that can be inflated outside of the helicopter," she says. "But it's not

When scientists find a site that might be good for a station, they land a helicopter on the ice and check out the site.

something I worry about too much because when we're traveling up there, there's ice around for the helicopter to land on. So if we're in trouble, the helicopter would land on the ice, and then we'd have to wait for the ship to come and get us." Pushing through the ice, the ship could take a couple of days to reach them, she admits. That is why the helicopter carries survival gear. "We are very alone up there. We're completely dependent on ourselves."

When the scientists spot a good site for a station, they land to check it out, and then return to the ship. The ship plows its way to the site. But the scientists do not just jump onto the floe, Hutchings says. The deck is 30 feet (9 km) or more above the surface of the ice. For safety, the ship lowers and lifts people onto and off the floe with a boxlike basket attached to a crane.

One of the things that the scientists do on the floes is drill holes through the ice to measure its thickness. A floe can be several yards thick. They also drill out long, four-inch-wide rods of ice called cores. By measuring the saltiness and temperature at different points along the core, Hutchings says she can learn how old the ice is and how quickly it has been melting. By comparing the data with core measurements from the year before, she can tell whether the current summer has been warmer or cooler.

Making a Winter Camp

Winter visits are much different. In midwinter, a team in a small airplane flies out over the Beaufort ice pack to find a campsite. "They want to find a nice, strong piece of ice that's very old to put the camp on. Next to it they need to find a piece of very new ice that's flat," Hutchings says. The flat ice is needed for a runway, so a plane can land with building materials to set up a cluster of huts and fly in the scientists and supplies.

The winter camp is built for the US Navy, which does its own Arctic research for military purposes. The camp is set to house up to sixty Navy researchers. After the

The US Navy Ice Camp Nautilus was built on a sheet of ice adrift on the Arctic Ocean off the coast of Alaska. The US Navy decided to dismantle the temporary ice camp a week earlier than planned after cracks appeared in the ice and made it too risky to use airfields to ferry people and supplies.

Navy has used the camp for several weeks, it allows other research groups to use it. Hutchings says about thirty scientists occupy the camp, along with seven support workers who cook, maintain the camp, and do other support work. At the end of winter, the camp is taken apart and flown back to land.

Late winter is bitterly cold with little daylight, Hutchings says. But the days begin to lengthen rapidly around the spring equinox in March. An equinox is a moment when the Sun is directly aligned with Earth's equator. On an equinox day, everywhere in the world sees nearly the same amount of daylight and darkness. "That far north, when you go through the equinox, you go very quickly from very long nights to very long days," she says. The reverse happens around the fall equinox.

The camp is not fancy. The huts are plain but insulated. They are heated with small oil stoves. Ice must be melted to make water for drinking and washing. And everyone must keep an eye out for polar bears. Hutchings says she has not seen a bear at an ice camp, but she has seen their tracks. Away from camp, people travel in groups for safety. They carry a flare gun to scare off an approaching bear and a rifle in case of an attack. Hutchings says it would take a well-aimed shot to stop a polar bear and she would not shoot one unless her life was at stake.

Her visits only last about two weeks. Like many other scientists, she works long hours to make the most of her time there. It is just as well, she says. It keeps her mind off the rough living conditions. "You're working so hard, you don't realize how rough it is. . . . You don't spend much time in your quarters. And we would be out up to 10 or 12 hours a day in the field. It's very intense."

Hutchings' specialty is studying the motions of the ice pack. For example, she has set up special instruments in different places on the ice. Each instrument uses satellite signals to measure the exact location of the ice. Each one also has a satellite telephone link to a computer. Every

Scientists and researchers working in the Arctic region must look out for polar bears. With the loss of sea ice, these animals are also losing food sources, and they are more likely to attack humans when hungry.

Sea Ice and Climate

Sea ice keeps the Arctic region cooler by reflecting sunlight back into space. Its bright surface reflects 80 percent of the sunlight that strikes it. In contrast, ocean water absorbs 90 percent of the sunlight that strikes it.

As saltwater freezes, the salt goes out of it. This makes the water around the ice saltier and denser, causing it to sink. The cold, dense polar water moves along the ocean bottom toward the equator, while warmer water above it moves toward the poles. Scientists call this circulation a "conveyor belt" that helps regulate global temperatures.

Sea ice forms a layer between water and air. It slows the transfer of heat from the ocean into the atmosphere. This results in lower air temperatures in the polar regions. Hutchings says the big difference in temperatures between the cold polar regions and the warm tropics is largely responsible for the weather patterns in North America. Changes in polar temperatures could change these patterns "dramatically," she says.

Storms, tides, and other forces put sea ice under stress and cause violent cracking. The cracks expose open water to the polar air. This allows heat to escape into the air. If the cracks stay open, new ice will form. If they close, they may form thick ridges of ice. Hutchings wants to know if changes in weather patterns on the Beaufort Sea will cause more cracks and ridges and whether the result will be more or less ice. She says this knowledge could help scientists predict how quickly a warming world might cause the summer ice pack to disappear.[6]

day, each instrument calls in its location from the distant pack ice. Hutchings has been using the instruments to track the movement of the pack ice.

An Icy Dip

In winter, it is easy to forget that the thick pack ice is not solid ground. Hutchings nearly lost her life once when she was literally driven through the ice into the ocean.

Hutchings was conducting an experiment to measure the opening and closing of leads. A lead opened half a mile from the camp, and she set up instruments around it that used satellite signals to measure their locations as the crack widened and narrowed.

But another lead in the ice pack almost did her in.

Hutchings says she was riding on the back of a snowmobile. "The driver decided that the flat ice on the lead in front of us would be very nice to travel on," Hutchings recalls. She says she warned the driver earlier that lead ice was often thin and unsafe.

The driver headed for it anyway. The surface of the lead ice was about a foot lower than the pack ice. The snowmobile, a heavy-duty machine, dropped onto the lead ice and broke through. The sled it was pulling went in with it.

"The next thing I knew, I was up to my waist in water, and then, I remember, the snow machine was sinking down underneath me. I grabbed hold of the sled . . . and then the sled was sinking, and I couldn't hold onto it anymore." Hutchings grabbed the edge of the pack ice, but it was a foot above the water and slippery. "A lot of people who fall in leads often don't get out because you can't pull yourself out," she says.

This incident illustrates another reason why people in ice camps travel in groups. Two other scientists were with them on another snowmobile, and they quickly pulled out Hutchings and the driver. They were two miles (three kilometers) from camp, and Hutchings' heavy snowsuit was soaked. But she says the outer layer froze and blocked the wind, so she stayed warm inside until she could get into her hut and put on dry clothes.

Hutchings continued with her work, but she admits the experience was scary. "After that, I went out into the field only when I absolutely had to. I was quite shook

A snowmobile pulls a sled with supplies. Hutchings had a frightening experience when the snowmobile she was riding went through the ice, along with the sled. She was lucky to surivive the ordeal.

up, actually. I had nightmares that there would be a lead opening up underneath the camp."

Hutchings says accidents like hers are rare, and she has continued to go to the ice camps. But she says she learned a valuable lesson: Choose a field companion who cares about safety, accepts advice, and watches out for others.

Dreaming of Antarctica

Hutchings's interest in science runs in the family. Her father is a chemist. Her interest in sea ice was sparked at age eight by her visit to the *Discovery*, the sailing ship used by British explorer Robert Falcon Scott to reach Antarctica in 1902. "It was moored in London and my mother took me to see it," she remembers. "Then I started reading about Captain Scott and Amundsen and their race to the South Pole." Norwegian polar explorer Roald Amundsen led the first successful expedition to the South Pole, reaching it in 1911. Scott reached it in 1912, but he and his four companions died on their return trip. Reading these historical tales of polar journeys captured her imagination. "Ever since then, I've been fascinated by the South Pole and Antarctica and the polar regions," Hutchings says.

She decided the best way to reach Antarctica was to become a scientist and go there for research. Her first step was deciding to study physics in college. "It was such a broad subject that I thought it would give you the tools you need to understand anything in the world."

But her work took her to the top of the world, not the bottom. After earning a bachelor of science degree in physics at the University College in London in 1995, she was offered a chance to work on her doctorate with someone who studied sea ice. This sparked an interest in the Arctic region that has become the focus of her work. "I've never got to Antarctica," she says with a laugh. She received a PhD in physics from the University College in London in 1999.

After working as a postdoctoral research fellow, Hutchings went into teaching physics at Oregon State University in Corvallis, where she is an assistant professor. Professors teaching at that level at a public college earned an average salary of $74,700 in 2013.[7]

Although her adventures on the ice sound thrilling, Hutchings says that is not what drives her. She spends a great deal of time teaching, analyzing data, writing reports, and seeking grants for research projects. Hutchings says she enjoys coming to an ever-greater understanding of how sea ice and climate are related.

Hutchings not only feels personal satisfaction from the knowledge she gains through her research, she also knows that her work is part of something bigger. She knows that every discovery she makes contributes to the larger body of scientific knowledge. "It's very satisfying to realize that [with] each small step you make, and each small question you answer, you're enhancing all of humanity's understanding of how the climate works. And it might be a very small step, but I think it's always important."

Appendix: Severe-Storm Scientists: Jobs at a Glance[1]

METEOROLOGIST	
Education Required	Bachelor's degree in physics, chemistry, or math, master's degree or PhD are sometimes required
Salary Range*	$50,000 to $130,000
PHYSICIST	
Education Required	Bachelor's degree in physics, master's degree or, preferably, PhD and postdoctoral research
Salary Range	$55,000 to $182,000
OCEANOGRAPHER	
Education Required	Bachelor's degree in geology, physics, or chemistry, master's degree, PhD for high-level position
Salary Range	$39,000 to $113,000
RESEARCH SCIENTIST	
Education Required	Bachelor's degree in physics, math, or related field, master's degree, PhD and postdoctoral research high-level position
Average Salary	$94,000
PHYSICS PROFESSOR	
Education Required	Bachelor's degree in physics, master's degree or, preferably, PhD, two to six years as postdoctoral scholar is common
Salary Range	$45,000 to $148,000
METEOROLOGY PROFESSOR	
Education Required	Bachelor's degree in physics, chemistry or math, master's degree or, preferably, PhD, two to six years as postdoctoral scholar is common
Salary Range	$42,000 to $149,000

[1] Bureau of Labor Statistics, *Occupational Outlook Handbook, 2014–15 Edition*, May 2013, US Department of Labor, http://www.bls.gov/oes/current/oes_stru.htm.

*Salary figures will vary according to job specifications, geographic location, and market demands.

Chapter Notes

Chapter 1. Chasing Knowledge

1. Personal interview with Joshua Wurman, January 25, 2007. Unless otherwise noted, all quotes from Wurman come from this interview.

Chapter 2. Nature's Fury

1. Personal interview with Joshua Wurman, January 25, 2007. Unless otherwise noted, all quotes from Wurman come from this interview.

2. "The Historic Forecast," *National Oceanic and Atmospheric Administration*, accessed February 2, 2015, <http://www.outlook.noaa.gov/tornadoes/torn50.htm>.

3. "Tornadoes: Nature's Most Violent Storms," *National Oceanic and Atmospheric Administration*, last modified August 2010, <http://www.crh.noaa.gov/lmk/preparedness/tornado_small/index.php>.

4. Personal interview with Joshua Wurman, and "What Is 'Tornado Alley'?" *Windows to the Universe*, accessed February 3, 2015, <http://www.windows2universe.org/earth/Atmosphere/tornado/alley.html>.

5. "Doppler Radar: Introduction," *National Weather Service*, last modified January 5, 2010, <http://www.srh.noaa.gov/srh/jetstream/doppler/doppler_intro.htm>.

6. Jason Samenow, "Deadly El Reno, Okla. Tornado Was Widest Ever Measured on Earth, Had Nearly 300 mph Winds," *Washington Post*, June 4, 2013, <http://www.washingtonpost.com/blogs/capital-weather-gang/wp/2013/06/04/deadly-el-reno-okla-tornado-was-widest-ever-measured-on-earth-

had-nearly-300-mph-winds>; Jason Samenow, "The Rare 'Anticyclonic' Tornado in El Reno, Okla.; Not Its First Encounter," *Washington Post*, June 5, 2013, <http://www.washingtonpost.com/blogs/capital-weather-gang/wp/2013/06/05/the-rare-anticyclonic-tornado-in-el-reno-okla/>.

7. University Corporation for Atmospheric Research, "The Road to Doppler Data," *UCAR Quarterly*, Summer 2003, <http://www.ucar.edu/communications/quarterly/summer03/doppler.html>.

8. Bureau of Labor Statistics, "Atmospheric and Space Scientists," *Occupational Outlook Handbook, 2014–2015 Edition*, May 2013, <http://www.bls.gov/oes/current/oes192021.htm>.

9. "Career Options for Meteorologists," *National Severe Storms Laboratory—NOAA*, accessed February 27, 2015, <http://www.nssl.noaa.gov/people/jobs/careers.php>.

10. Joshua Wurman, "Joshua Wurman CV," *Center for Severe Weather Research,* 2013, <http://cswr.org/contents/wurman-cv-2013.pdf>.

Chapter 3. A Storm Lab in the Mountains

1. Personal interview with Anna Gannet Hallar, September 6, 2007. Unless otherwise noted, all quotes from Hallar come from this interview.

2. Desert Research Institute, "Welcome to Storm Peak Laboratory," *Storm Peak Laboratory,* accessed February 3, 2015, <http://stormpeak.dri.edu>.

3. Ibid.

4. D. Obrist, A.G. Hallar, and I. McCubbin, "Mercury Monitoring at Storm Peak Laboratory in Colorado to Determine Regional and Asian Long-Range Transport Contributions to

Atmospheric Mercury Loads," presented at the International Conference on Air Quality, Arlington, Va., September 2007, abstract via e-mail from Hallar, October 10, 2007.

5. Anna Gannet Hallar, "Reflections on My Undergraduate Internship Opportunity," *Internships: A Taste of the Working World*, Truman State University Career Center, April 9, 2003.

6. "McMurdo Station," *National Science Foundation, Directorate for Geosciences*, accessed February 3, 2015, <http://www.nsf. gov/geo/plr/support/mcmurdo.jsp>.

7. "Your Stay at McMurdo Station Antarctica," *National Science Foundation, Office of Polar Programs, NASA Quest*, accessed February 3, 2015, <http://quest.nasa.gov/antarctica/ background/NSF/mc-stay.html>.

8. Melinda Mawdsley, "Office With a View: New Scientists Take Over Operation of Storm Peak Laboratory," *Steamboat Today*, November 24, 2006, <http://www.steamboatpilot. com/news/2006/nov/24/office_view/>.

9. "Dr. Gannet Hallar," *Desert Research Institute*, accessed February 3, 2015, <http://www.dri.edu/directory/4874-gannet-hallar>.

Chapter 4. Alaska's Wild Weather

1. "Brown Bear," *Alaska Department of Fish and Game*, January 2015, <http://www.adfg.alaska.gov/index.cfm?adfg=brownbear. main>.

2. Personal interview with Gary Hufford, March 22, 2007. Unless otherwise noted, all quotes from Hufford come from this interview.

3. "UAF Facts and Figures," *University of Alaska Fairbanks*, September 2013, <http://www.uaf.edu/facts/>.

4. Lenny Bernstein et al., *Climate Change 2007: Synthesis Report,* Intergovernmental Panel on Climate Change, November 2007, p. 8, <http://www.ipcc.ch/pdf/assessment-report/ar4/syr/ar4_syr.pdf>.

5. Richard B. Alley et al., "Summary for Policymakers," *Climate Change 2007: The Physical Science Basis,* Intergovernmental Panel on Climate Change, Paris, February 5, 2007, <https://www.ipcc.ch/publications_and_data/ar4/wg1/en/spm.html>; Lisa V. Alexander et al., "Summary for Policymakers," *Climate Change 2013: The Physical Science Basis,* Intergovernmental Panel on Climate Change, Paris, 2013, <https://www.ipcc.ch/pdf/assessment-report/ar5/wg1/WG1AR5_SPM_FINAL.pdf>.

6. "Climate Change in Alaska," *State of Alaska,* December 2011, <http://www.climatechange.alaska.gov>.

7. Ibid.

8. "Pay and Leave," *US Office of Personnel Management,* January 2015, <http://www.opm.gov/policy-data-oversight/pay-leave/salaries-wages/salary-tables/15Tables/html/AK.aspx>; "FAQ: Employment in Meteorology," *National Weather Service,* April 17, 2014, <http://www.srh.noaa.gov/oun/?n=faq-employment>.

Chapter 5. Into the Eye of a Hurricane

1. "Frequently Asked Questions," *Atlantic Oceanographic and Meteorological Laboratory, Hurricane Research Division,* July 25, 2011, <http://www.aoml.noaa.gov/hrd/tcfaq/A1.html>.

2. CNN Library, "Hurricane Katrina Statistics Fast Facts," *CNN. com,* August 22, 2014, <http://www.cnn.com/2013/08/23/us/hurricane-katrina-statistics-fast-facts/index.html>.

3. "Hurricane Rita," *National Climatic Data Center,* September 22, 2005, <http://www.ncdc.noaa.gov/extremeevents/specialreports/Hurricane-Rita2005.pdf>.

4. Eric S. Blake, Christopher W. Landsea, and Ethan J. Gibney, "The Deadliest, Costliest and Most Intense United States Tropical Cyclones From 1851 to 2010," *National Weather Service, NOAA Technical Memorandum NWS NHC-6,* August 2011, <http://www.nhc.noaa.gov/pdf/nws-nhc-6.pdf>.

Chapter 6. Unlocking Lightning's Mysteries

1. Personal interview with Earle Williams, April 4, 2007. Unless otherwise noted, all quotes from Williams come from this interview.

2. "Lightning Basics," *NOAA, National Severe Storms Laboratory,* accessed February 3, 2015, <http://www.nssl.noaa.gov/education/svrwx101/lightning/>.

3. "Lightning: Just for Kids," *University Center for Atmospheric Research,* April 4, 2000, <http://www.ucar.edu/communications/infopack/lightning/kids.html>.

4. "Report of Investigation: Fatal Underground Coal Mine Explosion," *US Department of Labor, Mine Safety and Health Administration,* accessed February 3, 2015, <http://www.msha.gov/Fatals/2006/Sago/sagoreport.asp>.

5. "Understanding the Lightning Threat: Minimizing Your Risk," *National Weather Services,* accessed February 3, 2015, <http://www.lightningsafety.noaa.gov/overview.htm>.

6. Ibid.

7. Ibid.

8. "2013 AAUP Faculty Salary Survey," *Chronicle of Higher Education*, April 8, 2013, <http://chronicle.com/article/2013-AAUP-Faculty-Salary/138291/>.

Chapter 7. Climate Clues in Sea Ice

1. Personal interview with Jennifer Hutchings, October 18, 2007. Unless otherwise noted, all quotes from Hutchings come from this interview.

2. National Snow and Ice Data Center, "Arctic Sea Ice Shatters All Previous Record Lows," press release, October 1, 2007, <http://nsidc.org/news/newsroom/2007_seaiceminimum/20071001_pressrelease.html>.

3. K. E. Trenberth et al., "Observations: Surface and Atmospheric Climate Change," *Climate Change 2007: The Physical Science Basis, Contribution of Working Group I to the Fourth Assessment Report of the Intergovernmental Panel on Climate Change*, Cambridge University Press, p. 239, accessed February 3, 2015, <http://www.ipcc.ch/pdf/assessment-report/ar4/wg1/ar4-wg1-chapter3.pdf>; T. F. Stocker et al., eds., *IPCC, 2013: Climate Change 2013: The Physical Science Basis. Contribution of Working Group I to the Fifth Assessment Report of the Intergovernmental Panel on Climate Change,* Cambridge University Press, p. 121, accessed February 3, 2015, <http://www.ipcc.ch/pdf/assessment-report/ar5/wg1/WG1AR5_Chapter01_FINAL.pdf>.

4. National Snow and Ice Data Center, "Introduction," *All About Sea Ice*, 2014, <http://nsidc.org/cryosphere/seaice/index.html>.

5. Luc Rainville, "It's the Ship!" *Beaufort Gyre Exploration Project*, July 26, 2007, <http://www.whoi.edu/page.do?pid= 67496>.

6. Ibid.

7. "2013 AAUP Faculty Salary Survey," *Chronicle of Higher Education*, April 8, 2013, <http://chronicle.com/article/2013-AAUP-Faculty-Salary/138291/>.

Glossary

Beaufort Gyre—A swirling pattern of Arctic water that traps sea ice. Ice floes drifting in the gyre may stay frozen for several years, clumping together to form pack ice.

boundary layer—A layer of air next to an object's surface. In weather science, it is the layer of the atmosphere closest to Earth's surface.

climate—The average weather for a given place over a long period of time.

diversity—Having people who are different genders, ethnic backgrounds, or who have different cultures in a group or organization.

Doppler radar—A type of radar used to study weather. By bouncing radio signals off raindrops, bugs, or dust carried in wind, a Doppler radar unit can measure the wind's speed and direction.

electrostatic charge—A buildup of electrons in an object so that it contains more electrons than a nearby object.

equinox—The moment when the Sun is lined up directly with Earth's equator. Earth has an equinox twice each year: one in the spring, around March 20, and one in the autumn, around September 23. On an equinox day, every place on Earth gets nearly the same amount of daylight and darkness.

eyewall—A tight wall of cloud ringing the clear center, or eye, of a hurricane.

eyewall replacement cycle—The process by which rain bands in a hurricane sometimes tighten around an eyewall to form a new eyewall, which chokes off and replaces the inner eyewall.

Faraday cages—Metal cages or boxes that protect people inside them from electricity. They work because the electric current flows across the outer surface. Faraday cages are named after British physicist Michael Faraday, a pioneer in the understanding of electricity.

floes—Pieces of sea ice.

free troposphere—A section of the lower atmosphere that lies above the boundary layer.

global circuit—An electric circuit that surrounds Earth, created by a positive electric charge in the upper atmosphere and a negative charge in Earth's surface.

global warming—A rising trend in the average temperature of Earth's surface. Scientists around the world say global warming is being caused by human activities, mainly by raising the level of carbon dioxide in the atmosphere.

greenhouse gas—A gas that traps heat as a greenhouse does. Carbon dioxide, water vapor, and methane are natural greenhouse gases. Human activities have increased carbon dioxide in the atmosphere by burning fuels that contain carbon, mainly coal and oil.

hurricanes—Tropical storms with winds of 74 miles (119 kilometers) per hour or greater, usually accompanied by rain, thunder, and lightning.

leads—Stretches of open seawater formed when pieces of sea ice cracks open.

lightning rods—Metal rods that are placed on a building and connected with the ground to protect the building from being damaged by lightning.

McMurdo Station—The largest outpost in Antarctica. It belongs to the United States.

meteorologists—Scientists who study weather. Meteorologists usually have at least a bachelor's degree in meteorology, the study of weather.

oceanography—The field of science that deals with the ocean.

pack ice—Drifting sea ice that has packed together in large masses.

permafrost—A permanently frozen layer of ground.

radar—A device that sends out radio waves for detecting and locating an object by the reflection of the radio waves and that may use this reflection to find out the position and speed of the object.

rain bands—Bands of heavy rain and wind that spiral outward from the center of a hurricane.

sea ice—Ice that is formed when ocean water freezes.

tornado—A violent, rotating column of air that reaches from a thunderstorm to the ground.

turbulence—An irregular motion of air that causes a plane to shake when in flight.

typhoons—Hurricanes that form in the western Pacific Ocean.

Further Reading

Books

Basher, Simon. *Climate Change*. London: Kingfisher, 2015.

Bright, Michael. *Weather Explained*. New York: Rosen, 2015.

Challoner, Jack. *Hurricane and Tornado*. New York: DK, 2014.

Hubbard, Ben. *Tornado*. Chicago: Heinemann, 2014.

Miller, Ron. *Chasing the Storm: Tornadoes, Meteorology, and Weather Watching*. Minneapolis: Twenty-First Century Press, 2014.

Videos

Chasing Ice. DVD. Directed by Jeff Orlowski. Exposure/Diamond Docs, 2012. 75 mins.

Join photographer James Balog as he travels to the Arctic in a quest to find out the truth about global warming.

Storm Chasers: Greatest Storms. DVD. Discovery, 2012. 172 mins.

Watch Dr. Josh Wurman and other storms chasers as they get up close with tornadoes, lightning, and all kinds of extreme weather.

Web Sites

c2es.org/science-impacts/basics/kids

Learn all about climate change and what can be done about it.

skydiary.com/kids/

Find out everything you want to know about tornadoes, lightning, hurricanes, and storm chasing.

scied.ucar.edu/webweather

Explore the different kinds of weather and what causes them.

Index